dreamseeds

A collection of poems
m.j. flores

Printed in Victoria, Canada

Note for Librarians: a cataloguing record for this book that includes Dewey Classification and US Library of Congress numbers is available from the National Library of Canada. The complete cataloguing record can be obtained from the National Library's online database at: www.nlc-bnc.ca/amicus/index-e.html

ISBN 1-4120-2171-5

TRAFFORD

This book was published on-demand in cooperation with Trafford Publishing.
On-demand publishing is a unique process and service of making a book available for retail sale to the public taking advantage of on-demand manufacturing and Internet marketing. On-demand publishing includes promotions, retail sales, manufacturing, order fulfilment, accounting and collecting royalties on behalf of the author.

Suite 6E, 2333 Government St., Victoria, B.C. V8T 4P4, CANADA

Phone	250-383-6864	Toll-free 1-888-232-4444 (Canada & US)
Fax	250-383-6804	E-mail sales@trafford.com
Web site www.trafford.com		TRAFFORD PUBLISHING IS A DIVISION OF TRAFFORD HOLDINGS LTD.
Trafford Catalogue #03-2720		www.trafford.com/robots/03-2720.html

10   9   8   7   6   5   4   3   2

Dedication

This book is dedicated to everyone with a dream
and especially to my family and friends.

Table of Contents

Preface

There is a seed inside the soul that grows into dreams. It is filled with incredible potential and the power to change. It is composed of the beauty of life and awakens you to live. This is a dreamseed.

dreamseeds is a collection of poems I have harvested from the different perspectives, thoughts and reflections in my life. There are many things in this world to experience, and poetry provides me with an opportunity to listen and communicate with my soul.

The language of life is filled with conversations we are always trying to understand. Every day I am learning accomplishments and failures, good times and bad. It is this contrast which makes life an experience, and no matter what life goes on.

The roots of the past and blooms of tomorrow live within each dream. There are so many possibilities that we must make sure we plant ourselves in becoming all that we can be. May this collection of poems be a window of sunlight and provide you with a different view of the incredible scenery in this garden called life.

Caterpillars And Butterflies

Sometimes I am like
The caterpillars and the butterflies

Sometimes I believe
That I will surface and I shall rise

Sometimes I hunger
That my goals will reach me soon

Sometimes I feel scared
Like I'm hiding behind a cocoon

Sometimes I can change
Metamorphosis starts to take me

Sometimes I succeed
And I have emerged triumphantly

Sometimes I grow wings
And I'm able to reach for the skies

Sometimes I am like
The caterpillars and the butterflies

When The Sand And The Sea Kiss

Silver sands and serene sea
Blend between so beautifully

Waving waters wash away
As scattered stones surf and stray

Like lover's lips in love lock
The dreamer's dreams drift and dock

Married movements match in bliss
When the sand and the sea kiss

Troubled

The world's too heavy
For my shoulders
It's a wait too much to bear

Outside it's getting
Even colder
And inside still needs repair

Uncomfortable
There's no where to go
My fear is too strong to drape

I've turned my back
And all that I know
Is I'm looking to escape

I built my world
And it crashed on me
I was too weak to defend her

The end was near
As all I could see
Were the ruins of my surrender

Underneath An Umbrella Sky

Underneath an umbrella sky
My rubber boots are never dry

As clouds spill open they arouse
Raindrops hopping from house to house

With bright umbrellas do they dance
On tippy toes that lightly prance

Parading through the crowded streets
They march and bounce in rhythmic beats

And playing hopscotch on the ground
Puddles form and I jump around

Freely falling in luscious rains
A ripple smiles and all remains

Underneath an umbrella sky
Where rubber boots are never dry

While I Wait For No Reply

I keep expecting...

There would be an answer
To every question

That the mailbox would be full
Of love letters and kind words

That the phone would ring
And I would hear your voice

You'd be the messenger
With good news to supply

But my questions
Still have no answers

And the mailbox
Is always empty

And the phone
Has never rung

And I keep expecting
While I wait for no reply

The Hug

If I were the hug
That makes things all better
I'd never let you go

I would rest my head
Holding you forever
In dreams we'd live to know

Wordless conversations
As warm filled thoughts
Know exactly what to say

Upon the evening sun
That sweeps sad clouds
And the tears of rain away

Sheltered in your arms
Together we would be
Embraced in a comfort lifelong

If I were the hug
That makes things all better
I'd forget anything was wrong

Leaves Dancing In The Wind

The chivalrous wind tenderly weaves
Caressing the curves of autumn leaves

Dressed in her gown of yellow and red
The wind blows a kiss upon her head

He sweeps her off her feet and they fly
Through twists and twirls in the open sky

Footsteps float in a ballet of fire
Rising in lust and passion's desire

The courtship love falls in romance
When the wind and autumn leaves dance

...Dreams are the inventors of possibility.

Peer Pressure

Doing something
You usually wouldn't do

By impersonating
Someone who is not you

Dyslexia

dnatsrednu t'nac I semitemoS
daer I taht sgniht eht fo emoS
naem reven lliw 'tluaf' siht tuB
deeccus reven lliw I taht

redrah krow ot evah lliw I
erom dna erom ecitcarp ll'I dnA
ti fo gnah eht teg I ecnO
erofeb naht reisae s'tI

slaog ym timil ton seod tI
uoy ekil tsuj ma I esuaceB
ecneitap dna ecitcarp emos htiW
eusrup t'nac uoy gnihton s'erehT

...Do not take your perception of a few to judge many.

9

Idiosyncrasies

How you looked me in the eyes
Was when I began to see
The quirks I could recognize
Of love's eccentricity

I remember every laugh
And the little things you'd do
Unique like a photograph
Are my memories of you

For when you held me tightly
Smallest moments would reveal
The tender touch so mighty
Of the way you made me feel

Disposable Faces

You say you don't like the face you wear
Well let's see what we have in store
I have faces in different colors
Would you like to try on some more

They also come in different sizes
They look better than the face you own
They also come in different materials
How about plastic or silicone

Something to make you a bit nicer
Something that will bring out your eyes
Who cares if it's not who you are
Everyone hides behind their lies

You need new lips and also a nose
How about a brand new set of teeth
And while you're at it a new face
Who cares what you look like underneath

...Friends help you appreciate the beauty of life.

Bombs Made Of People

When the bombs made of people ignite
Anger explodes in conflicts to fight
And pieces torn between the wrong and right

Ignorance straps to vicious attacks
Triggers of terror bleed through the cracks
Violence erupts behind innocent backs

Injustice responsible for pain
Revenge compensates for those now slain
And crowded streets become morgues once again

As the bombs made of people increase
Fueled by hate can no suffering cease
But understanding frees the hostage peace

Catching Snowflakes On My Tongue

Chasing
The crystal sky

Full
Of flavorful snowflakes

Falling
Ever so gingerly

Icing
Like those of sugary cakes

Landing
Gently on tempted buds

Dissolving
Upon my tongue embraced

Catching
Snowflakes in my mouth

Savoring
Winter's delicious taste

...Do not get too comfortable in a place which makes you
forget your dreams.

Climbing Apple Trees On Autumn Days

Branches of the apple trees
Are fingers touching the sun
As restless leaves ride the breeze
Fall has ripened and begun

Climbing on each bough I cling
Moving like the monkeys do
With pendulum arms I swing
To find the greatest of view

Cradled in an apple tree
Of branches rustic and brown
Life is so different to see
When you're hanging upside down

Abortion

Troubled
She can't remember what she knew

Lost
She doesn't know what to do

Pain
Is all that her body can feel

Bruised
Mentally she is unable to heal

Scattered
Are the pieces in her mind

Nightmare
Of what she's left behind

Memory
Of a child's face she wouldn't see

Illusion
Of a child that will never be

Jealousy

Having something
That is not in my possession

Craving the desire
It becomes my obsession

I want it as much as it wants me
So much it becomes a need

Fueled by my selfish acts
I'm consumed by all my greed

Shy

I'm the one standing
With nervousness
And puppy dog eyes

Wishing for words
To stumble and approach
Rather than scared butterflies

I'd like to say hello
Hoping we'd get lost
In a facet of conversations

Than to still be waiting
For something to happen
Of untouched expectations

...God is the heartbeat of all things.

An Elephant's Missing Tail

When I was little

With the fascination of a three-year old
I cut out the picture of an elephant with glee

It was from the back of an old cereal box
And the bright colors seemed to captivate me

But somehow his tail accidentally fell off
And mistakenly into the trash was it thrown

I cried and I cried way past my bedtime
Thinking it was lost forever into the unknown

My parents would search through the garbage
Looking for the smallest remainder of a tail

And after a very long night they succeeded
As they glued it back with the greatest of detail

My elephant was now whole and complete
The same picture that I had cut out with glee

But I would learn and still can't comprehend
How much my parents really loved me

When I was little

Warm Socks

Naked toes
Curling and crawling

Into a cave
Of ticklish wool

Burrowing deep inside
Nudging corners

Fabric stretching
Oh! What a footful

But on a cold floor
On a frigid morning

Comfy warm socks
Nothing is more beautiful

...Differences accentuate similarities.

How My Heart Loves To Be Held In Your Hands

How my heart loves to be held in your hands
Caught from the seas flowing gently with grace
And anchored to shores of comforting lands
In the harbor of your soul's serene place

How my heart mirrors my true reflection
Like precious pearls that perpetually grow
Caressed in waters deep in affection
The many layers of love's friendship glow

As kindness glistens in candlelight gleams
Beneath liquid skies so calming and clear
Enclosed in the womb of passionate dreams
You bring the world to me that I hold dear

For you reach the depths my heart does contain
And bring them to surface, my love to reign

The Faces In The Clouds

Upon rich meadows brightened by day
I look above to where thoughts can play

Rolling hills revolve around skies
As softened clouds of cotton rise

The airy edges leave air brushed trails
Forming figures as nature exhales

Her breath is calm, patient and still
While she paints portraits at her will

And many impressions one can see
In the clouds' art of creativity

...Kind words echo, harsh words deafen.

Racism

Thoughts in appearances
Intolerant of the person inside

Differences discriminated
By being labeled and classified

When who we are is persuaded
Through prejudice point of view

By being painted in another color
That is different from you

Yelling

You make me feel so small
I cower down at your knees
My skin is covered in goose bumps
And I beg you to stop… please

Your anger hurts me deeply
My ears are burning in pain
My world has come crashing down
I don't think I can live again

Your frustration echoes my mind
You're not the same person I knew
And each time you yell at me
I become more and more afraid of you

…The most painful hurt is being hurt by someone you
trusted.

In A Cup Of Coffee

It has been so long since I have tasted
The warm touch of conversation on my tongue
And the flavorful words you always bring
Like the ones that reminisce when we were young

The fragrant smell still lingers in the air
As we indulge in our stories to be told
Having brewed through countless hours of past
They wait to be sipped at before they get cold

The delicious time we spend savoring
Leaves me wanting a refill on life's caffeines
Through the memories we've lived and tasted
Especially enjoyed when we spill the beans

Eulogy To A Friend

Each memory I hold lives in my heart
Underneath the past of yesterday's skies
Loyal is love that will never depart
Of the kindness and respect in your eyes

Gentle was each word, honest each embrace
Your presence as warm as the morning glow
To experience the smiles upon your face
Are soulful moments I cherish to know

For each gesture, each laugh, each caring touch
Reminds me of the love you would display
In every characteristic and such
Each memory I hold lives a new day

Now time may sleep as forever imparts
Dwelling in friendship rests eternal hearts

...Where there is faith, there is hope.

Bubbles

If I were a bubble drifting through the sky
I would rock in the wind and float really high

I'd touch the clouds as translucent colors prance
And see where reflections of rainbows all dance

As children would chase me with wondrous eyes
I'd listen to their smiles and giggling cries

They'd see magic and wonder they understand
Bursting into laughs by a very quick hand

Where suds and soaps and imagination double
Forming and flowing in the breath of a bubble

Famine

I hunger for a chance
A chance I might survive

Tomorrow I hope
That I might be alive

The heat beats down
And all our crops are dry

We live in a drought
With the fire in the sky

My flesh and my skin
Hang dearly to my bone

I hunger for some food
Some food of my own

And within each day
Conditions deprive

The chance to see tomorrow
A chance I might survive

...Perspective has many eyes; but it all depends on the ones
you choose to see with.

Homeless Sweet Homeless

The disposable lives
We overlook and throw away
Worthless of social class
Ignorance lives another day

Poverty's pregnancy
Is a child no one wants to bear
Another mouth to feed
Becomes a burden to welfare

Headlines of no respect
For children who have grown rotten
How life's less important
And wasted on the forgotten

Fairy Tale

Every girl is a princess
And every boy is a prince
And everybody lives
Happily ever since

Every woman is a queen
And every man is a king
That's the end of slavery
And the end of suffering

But we're not in a fairy tale
We have our right and wrong
But if we realize everyone is special
It would be easier to get along

For in that fairy tale
There are only cries of laughter
Because everybody lives
Happily ever after

… Encouragement keeps me swimming, even in the
undertow of disappointment.

I Opened Up A Star

In midnight sky speckled light
Originates from a single star

Perched in the dark depths of night
Endlessly staring distant and far

Nothing but the space between
Eludes us from touching each other

Dwelling in my heart I've seen
Universal love reach another

Peeling away the sections
As everything that sparkles so free

Shines in many directions
The existence that glistens in me

And always within every deepened night
Reaches a star that forever burn bright

Please Get Better

In those long nights
Where waiting is the only comfort
I'm so afraid of losing you

Watching you fight
Each time taking more and more effort
I pray hoping you'll soon pull through

Bedside flowers
And tubes like spaghetti make me scared
I clutch your hand not letting go

Sleepless hours
Unsure as time has me unprepared
Nervous feelings are all I know

Please get better
Because I just don't know what to do
I'm so afraid of losing you

I'm so afraid …of losing you

Armor Of Love

Let the gentle night sleep in late
For morning's hour is sure to wait

When upon your face moonlight falls
Sweet whispers echo heart felt calls

And staring at the star filled skies
Through constellations in your eyes

Beauty of tender souls undress
Wrapped in the warmth of love's caress

And woven in the arms of protection
Is the gentle armor of affection

She Bathes In Beauty Of Bounteous Seas

She bathes in beauty of bounteous seas
Where her footsteps touch and fondle the shore
Leaving impressions of love's memories
Within my heart her embrace I adore

Her skin is soft and her fragrance so sweet
Like a blooming bouquet of fresh flowers
The ecstasy as my heart skips a beat
Lingers forever in lasting hours

She is so precious and pretty to see
In the luminous light where friendship glows
And everything that I hold dear to me
Is in our love that continually flows

For as long as there breathes a day and night
This kiss from the soul will always unite

...The best way to see your dreams, is to close your eyes
and imagine.

Life

For every action
However strange

Counters a reaction
Causing change

Misconception

Often times it's easy to conceive
A false hope that we want to believe

Listening to words that we want to hear
And skipping the parts to which we fear

We carry our lies hoping they'll bear
Something that was never really there

For what we thought is all deception
And the stillborn of misconception

… Keep an open mind, for you are able to see further than
closed mind narrowed by walls and borders.

Somewhere To Cry

Sadness fills a sunken heart
Orphaned from a love's depart

Memories of yesterday
End in tears that seem to stay

When will I forget the pain
Having held the loss of gain

Evidence of thoughts I keep
Remains when I cry to sleep

Each passing hour feels so bare
Thoughts of you not being there

Opened wounds that never heal
Captured as the senses feel

Remembrance is a sad touch
Yesterday still hurts so much

I Am A Child

We are all children
With minds that explore
Observing with question
We learn something more

In our minds we can be
Whatever we please
We can choose to become
Whatever our imagination sees

Each day we are learning
Things we didn't know
But more importantly
We learn how we must grow

Never stop growing
Let your imagination run wild
And never stop learning
With the mind of a child

I am a child

Running Through Sprinklers

The staring sun
Never looks away
In the seething sky
Of humid day

Silhouette shadows
Prance on the ground
As children play
And frolic around

Running back and forth
Hopping in flight
The rain dance brings
Splashes of delight

The cool spray soothes
The prevalent heat
Running through sprinklers
Tickles my feet

Flying My Unstrung Kite

In the solace of a peaceful blue sky
The wet windowsills of my eyes now dry

Curfews no longer confine me to stay
In shadows of war where children can't play

Ribbons anchor to clouds like flags fly free
Bright colors replace those of casualty

Swept away from the tangles of violence
Hope rises for strength to end our silence

As the uniforms of the uninformed
Unite to understand peace must be formed

Without strings of war we reach greater heights
Flying like freedom and our unstrung kites

… Poetry is the reflection of my soul.

Gently Does My Heart Still Beat

Gently does my heart still beat
Songs of love that sing in me
Rhythms of life's symphony

Upon each breath that I greet
God gave me a chance to be
A note in eternity

Invisible

Again
I go unseen and
Never recognized

Again
It seems the world
Is too desensitized

Again
I try to speak but
My voice goes unheard

Again
It seems the world is
Blind until it has occurred

Again

… Patience is the skill that takes the longest time to learn.

Loneliness Is The Lost Island

Loneliness is the lost island
Waiting to be discovered and found

The landscape of a lonely place
That shares with no one being around

Loneliness is the lost location
Feelings of being unwanted compound

As the landscape of a lonely face
Cries in the tears of an island that drowned

As Day Moved On

I stood and watched the sunset
Calmly fade into the night
The horizon disappeared
As darkness devoured light

I stood and watched all the stars
Calmly blink their tranquil eyes
The horizon reappeared
In the morning of sunrise

I could not wait forever
Because time kept passing by
And the past I could not change
As day moved on, so must I

...Sometimes our biggest problem is making small
problems seem too big and challenging.

The Fossils Of Childhood

In sandboxes where early moments remained
The past is a fossil when childhood once reigned

I sifted through stories and sweet lullabies
Uncovering wishes in the night time skies

Boats would be floating in puddles on the street
Next to lemonade stands so sugary sweet

Piggyback rides made me feel giant and tall
Like building snowmen after the first snowfall

I would roll down the hills and fly with my kite
And snuggle next to my teddy bear at night

I'd spin dizzily on the merry-go-round
And look at the curious things that I found

I'd expose history before I understood
While excavating the fossils of childhood

Sunflowers

Like giants they stretch into the skies
With necks that peak above garden walls

And leafy limbs colossal in size
Hang loosely in the faint wind that sprawls

Their golden crowns reflect the hours
Tanned in the light an ample face blooms

Filled with life and of future flowers
Seeds hug together in tiny wombs

The warm day illuminates the skies
In the morning when sunflowers rise

… Life lives only in the present.

In The Field Of Mines

In the field of mines
Where war's seeds are sown

I cautiously place
My steps where I've known

As the roots of violence
Burrow deep in the ground

You don't want to harvest
Any plants you have found

For in uprooted soils
Broken bones dismember

Farmed are the missing limbs
A meal you remember

Crops never gather
Death is only grown

In the field of mines
Where war's seeds are sown

Support

You cripple my chances for trying
When negative words are all I hear
They make me feel like a failure
And it's become the only thing I fear

You criticize all of my decisions
Without letting me act for my own
You are the sticks and stones
That have pierced and broken my bones

Instead of always putting me down
With words that hurt and offend
Instead of being like an enemy
Could you try being more like a friend

... I am the only one who can change me.

Tiny Ants

I see them scurry
And march on the ground
Their tiny footsteps
Hardly make a sound

Moving with gusto
There's many to see
Crawling and searching
In community

The tiniest world
Seems giant and grand
As I watch them build
Their castles of sand

The wonder I feel
Each time I recall
The greatness of life
In an ant so small

Season Of Death

Time invited me to stay
But life was ready to leave
There was no more time to play
And no more time to grieve

Eternity held my hand
I glanced to the other side
It wasn't how I had planned
But I would not decide

As I said goodbye she waved
Fading into the distance
Holding memories I saved
Remained of my existence

I looked back to where I was
And arrived with my last breath
The seasons changed to because
As I introduced to death

… As long as people have opinions, you can't please
everybody.

Season Of Life

Time invited me to stay
He gave me life to borrow
I would have the chance to play
And live for tomorrow

Experience taught me well
I was born within a dream
Potential will always tell
Life is what it may seem

My opened eyes looked ahead
There was just so much to do
With ambition I was lead
With the life I would walk through

How powerful life can be
The labor you make worthwhile
But as seasons change to see
Life is precious and fragile

Bullied

Teased

Torment is the only friend I've known

Picked on

Insult can never leave me alone

Pushed around

Why must I always be humiliated

Haunting

Pain keeps me constantly intimidated

No more

Pretending in this world of false glory

Silence screams

Dear mom and dad I'm so very sorry…

Let Us Waltz Through Fields Of Dandelion Seas

Let us waltz through fields of dandelion seas
Salaciously swept by the saltant breeze

And fall in the arms of gentle caress
Where all the senses feel love's luminesce

For to touch your soul is to touch the sun
As you bring me life and you make me one

Let us fall asleep beneath lustrous skies
Where kaleidoscope dreams rest in your eyes

Teacher

You don't have to be great
To teach the things that you know

You don't need to be famous
To help someone grow

You don't have to be rich
To give knowledge and education

You don't have to be a genius
To provide a truthful explanation

You do have to be someone
Who will try their best and yearn

To help someone else
Able to understand and learn

...My failures have been the foundations of my successes.

Discouragement

I tried and tried
Was it not meant to be

Why are there no signs
It's not helping me

Everyone seems
To be getting somewhere

So why am I lost
And not any where

Sterile trees of success
Bare no results

And all my attempts
Just feel like insults

It gets so much harder
How to prevail

When all my actions
Have led me to fail

Let's Pretend

Let's pretend
We're all super heroes
Let's pretend
That no one has to defend
Let's pretend
There's no fighting or war
Let's pretend
Everyone is a friend

Let's pretend
We all love each other
Let's pretend
Everyone can get along
Let's pretend
Everyone is equal
Let's pretend
We can all sing the same song

Let's pretend
There's no famine or hunger
Let's pretend
All argument will cease
Let's pretend
That there is only friendship
Let's pretend
Everyone is in peace

Let's pretend

In Lily Ponds Where Dragons Fly

In lily ponds where dragons fly
And castle clouds float in the sky

The damsel of dawn dresses bright
In the rich rays of morning light

She stares from her room high above
Patiently waiting for her love

He is her knight who'll save the day
Where in his arms she'll gently lay

Safe from the skies where dragons fly
Asleep in dreams and lullaby

My Imaginary Friend

We hang around one another
I think you're my very best friend
We can depend on each other
Until our friendship turns pretend

For you wear so many faces
It's hard to see through your disguise
When conformity replaces
Any truth soon turns into lies

And now you don't even see me
Since I never followed the trend
Popularity ignores me
Like my imaginary friend

… True friends love you not when you are at your greatest,
but when you are at your weakest.

Sea Turtles

I watched as a sea turtle laid her eggs
As she climbed out from the surf and the tide
Her behemoth body was without legs
Yet patiently she would crawl with each stride

And upon the shore she lifted her head
And burrowed a womb deeply in the sand
Then she would tuck her children into bed
With love mother sea turtles understand

Puberty

His build was small and slender
His face was clean and bare
But that was before I noticed him
Before I really had to stare

Clothes like attitudes had changed
And he gained a much bigger body
Housing the lack of maturity
Anxious to show everybody

Hair showed up in unexpected places
The voice I once knew was in danger
As the tickle in my throat subsided
With the voice of a new stranger

... Tragedy reminds us what is really important.

Unfulfilled

It hasn't gone the way that I planned
Or with answers I can understand

For the questions of what if collide
In different choices I could decide

And lost in the meaning I don't know
If significance will ever show

If there is purpose then where am I
If there is reason please tell me why

Ordinary Moments

Before I realized...

It seemed so ordinary
And familiar to occur

But...

Those times are no longer here
And I long for the days that were

Before I remembered...

How precious and how special
Each moment would aver

How much I miss them...

Now that they're gone

Your Meaningless Words

Promises of words
Are better left unsaid
Than false hopes I had
That were much too overfed

Were you not listening
To what you had to say
Or you just didn't care
As long as you got your way

You promised to call
But no answer was heard
Only the selfish response
Of your meaningless words

Heroes

They are those faces our memories keep
Who we looked up to with admiring eyes

Whose eternal presence will never sleep
They are the difference that helps us to rise

They are the supports which make us stronger
With encouragement that will never mar

Every hope is a dream that lives longer
And inspires us to become who we are

Noble is love where altruism thrives
In every day heroes who change our lives

... The greatest respect is given to those who give it the
most.

Sandwiches Without The Crust

In elementary years
I remember a lunch bag

Packed with a sandwich
Carved without the crust

And the kindly reminder
Of a mother's love

Unconditionally packed
Doing more than she must

Hurt

Abuse

Has lifted his heavy hand

Frightened

By answers I can't understand

Cornered

In weakness I shrivel and hide

Crying

To stop all this hurt deep inside

Taken

Advantaged by power too strong

Breaking

The silence always feels wrong

Mermaid Seas

We swam across clear waters blue
Where sunset seemed to follow you

Your long hair flowed and moved with grace
And anchored to your pretty face

As dolphins sailed between the tide
Seashells shuffled in hurried stride

To catch a glimpse of how you dressed
Swept by the beauty you expressed

And as coral reefs waved their hands
My tippy toes would touch the sands

I'd watch you dance beneath the sea
The mermaid of my reverie

The Big Guns Of Little Men

They like to feel big instead of being small
Equipped with their anger it makes them feel tall

Relentless and threatening violence wants more
Ravaging each other all they know is war

Outcomes of corruption aimlessly take life
Responsibilities become prisoners of strife

Intimidation and lies no truth can see
Scores of revenge in the graves of casualty

Many are the weapons that man can create
So sad is the construction of a man's hate

... The day is like a coin in a candy dispenser, for what you
get out of it—is how much you put in.

Spider Webs

Crystal threads
Spun together
With unique designs
Like translucent lace

And this arrangement
Is the home
Of the spider's
Resting place

Appearances
Can be deceiving
Stretching the truth
They grow wider

Until beauty like prey
Are trapped
In the tangled webs
Of the spider

When You Left Me

I slowly fell apart
I couldn't face the day
I became so nervous
I couldn't find my way

You never wanted me
You tossed me to the ground
You never really cared
If someday I would be found

No medicine will heal me
My heart is sore and bruised
I am weak and frightened
Feeling scared and used

My feathers are plucked
And I don't think I can fly
Except only fall down
Fall down and cry

When you left me

The Universe In My Bedroom

As a child my room became a universe
When I curled up in my bed and closed my eyes
As the night like a blanket wrapped around me
I began to see all the stars in the skies

My bed would transform into a rocket ship
To explore ideas that came out to play
The endless worlds I could seek out and visit
Were only a thinker's thought distance away

Fueled with courage and the passport of freedom
My thoughts became a map to what I could see
As I traveled the infinite universe
Of all the dreams in everything I could be

The Skipping Stones Of Heaven

The sky is a sea of sentient streams
Swimming with stars and of endlessness dreams

Each flame that flickers another burns bright
Carved from the darkness emerges the light

As sands mold mountains and earthly designs
A sculpture of stone and beauty entwines

Holding horizons of emerald and blue
There's so much to see in heavenly view

Earth is a pebble, a mere rock in sod
But a stone chosen in the hands of God

… What is life but an experience?

Speechless

The Fishing Trip

As the motors propelled us through the waters
We headed towards an inlet of the sea
We were fishing in our sailing boat
It was a moment spent with my old man and me

The scenery flashed through my eyes
While the misty water sprayed my face
I was a stranger to this territory
Like an astronaut visiting outer space

The trip was a bonding of love and memories
As both in time will continue to grow
We made the best of this adventurous journey
As you can only receive what you sow

As we waited patiently in anticipation
What would be the next meal on our dish
The excitement and pleasing surprise
That would come from one lonely fish

It was a fishing trip I wouldn't forget
Spending time with the old man for a day
Building memories and stories
Like the big one that got away

I felt a vibration surging through my rod
As I caught a moment and seized the day
I now have learned to catch a fish
And to not let the moment pass away

Invincible

It wasn't suppose to happen to me
I am too indestructible to ache

It only happens to everyone else
Until I find out there's been a mistake

I try to deny it but it's too late
How so easily I crumble and break

Why me

Marshmallow Moon

Beneath the clear of satin skies
Stars like freckles glimmer
As the full moon feasts on water
Pale reflections shimmer

Sugary mosquitoes
Are the brave hunters that explore
Armed with hungry sweet tooth's
They are always craving for more

From the flames of a roasting fire
Dissolving into night
Sweet stories and camp songs linger
Into memories of delight

And with fishing sticks carved
One will have no need for a spoon
To catch a scrumptious taste
Of the yummy marshmallow moon

… You find out how strong you really are when you are at
your weakest.

Plastic Smile

It's the false faces you wear
And images you buy
When the truth begins to tear
Through illusion and lie

It's makeup of make believe
And stories held by glue
Propaganda to perceive
Everything must be true

The appearances you sell
And masques of deception
Are all but a hollow shell
Without a reflection

Your real face I never see
For truth's never in style
It hurts like a cavity
Lodged in your plastic smile

For When Does Love Exist To Be

For when does love exist to be
Like waterfalls that flow so free
In hours of a romantic night
Or upon the first glance of sight

When sensuous smiles laugh with glee
And heaven shines with majesty
Or when the world now seems to hush
With all the words that make you blush

For when does love exist to be
The timeless time of unity
Within the soul which gently warms
As two hearts end and one heart forms

... Peace is the doorway of love, and the window of
compassion.

I Was Wrong

I wish I could make it all disappear
The sadness that serenades in your eyes

And make the past suddenly reappear
Before I was too late to realize

My actions hurt the trust you gave to me
As I fell far from the skies of glory

And your wounds left a haunting memory
I was wrong... and I'm so very sorry

A Passenger Staring Outside The Window

Staring outside the window
The scenery flashes by
I am just a passenger
Watching and wondering why

The newness of old places
And sights I don't recognize
Strange lands and different customs
Yet all beneath the same skies

Experiencing the same world
But with different thoughts we see
The many diverse windows
Like the views from inside me

… People keep taking advantage of everyone else, but not
too many people are taking advantage of themselves.

Addiction

She looked at me with her seductive smile
As temptation said it was worth my while

It was supposed to be a one-night stand
But my decision never went as planned

I couldn't let go and wanting to stay
I sold her my life and gave it away

And now our love is such strong conviction
My mistake of falling for addiction

Fragile

Defenseless to fend off fear
I'm so hesitant to try

After hurt was too severe
Again I don't want to cry

Agonized with worried eyes
Relationships I can't face

Too afraid to realize
The tears on my pillowcase

Vulnerable to hurt again
My fragile fears have spoken

As the shards that cut me then
Leave me forever broken

… Choice is the action of responsibility.

81

Unexpected

I trembled without thinking
You asked and I replied
Hesitant no answer
I was not ready to decide

The uncomfortable pause
My thoughts too much to weigh
And inexperienced words
Did not know what to say

All I had was question
For what was I to do
When unexpected waits
And is finally ready to meet you

Simple Things

Simple things seem to sparkle
When the light of your friendship shines

Like walking through the heavens
Amongst an angels' valentines

While collecting conversations
In bassinettes throughout the day

Every precious memory
I so carefully tuck away

… I don't know if the grass is greener on the other side, but
I do know my perception is.

Regrets

I regret not being there for you
I regret how time has passed us by
I regret the lies you heard
I regret about the times we'd cry

I regret the actions I chose
I regret not doing what I could
I regret how the past can't change
I regret not doing what I should

Through these regrets I now learn
That in the present I must take action
And delve myself in knowing that
I made an attempt to live in satisfaction

Baby Breath

In cradled arms and bundled love
The immortal dreams one dreams of

The tiny smiles memories keep
As newborn eyes emerge from sleep

Life's fragile face naked and bare
Is precious time that time may share

A baby's breath is breathtaking
When dreams are born and are waking

… The worst failure is to give up without even trying.

Morning Sun

If I were the morning sun
That rises into the day
I would brighten the whole world
And awaken all to play

I'd paint colors rich and free
In splashes of tender love
And watch and take care of you
Always ardent from above

I would be the light that shines
Touching the life in each one
Filled with the warmth of God's love
If I were the morning sun

Losing Touch

Once we were the best of friends
But not anymore today
I remember our friendship
Gradually fading away

I wondered if we gave up
The fight so small yet strong
Because it broke our friendship
And neither was right or wrong

I didn't do anything
To save the bond we once had
Not even give another chance
And it makes me feel so mad

To know what fun I would miss
And the memories I'd spend
Enjoying all the good times
Until I lost a good friend

... Sing the song within your heart and live.

Pillar of Triumph

Truest strength is being strong
When tragedy reifies
When you endure what is wrong
And you stand and you rise

When you conquer any fears
Your courage becomes true
And every hope perseveres
With the strength within you

You Left The Faucet Running

You left the faucet running again
How many times must I tell you
So when are you going to listen
To the things that I tell you what to do

Turn off the lights when they're not in use
Always wash your hands before you eat
Remember don't talk with your mouth full
And don't lose your temper in defeat

Always remember to brush and floss
Always remember to clean your plate
Don't forget to wash behind your ears
And always remember to participate

You left the faucet running again
How many times must I tell you
And I know it sounds mean sometimes
But I say it because I love you

... The best time to act and follow your dreams is now.

In A Treasure Box Of Yesterdays

In a treasure box of yesterdays
There were many special things I kept
And time the collector would appraise
All my recollections when I slept

Antique were my letters of living
And conversations of various themes
So valued was love that kept giving
And priceless were my pictures of dreams

Unique were all the moments I'd spend
Collecting the wonders of each day
And framing the fortunes of a friend
Upon the heavens where kindness lay

For life is but a treasure we hold
In experiences that time displays
Where memories are richer than gold
In a treasure box of yesterdays